Jazz Course for All Instruments

5 Simple Strategies for Developing Jazz Language and Fluency

Lukas Gabric

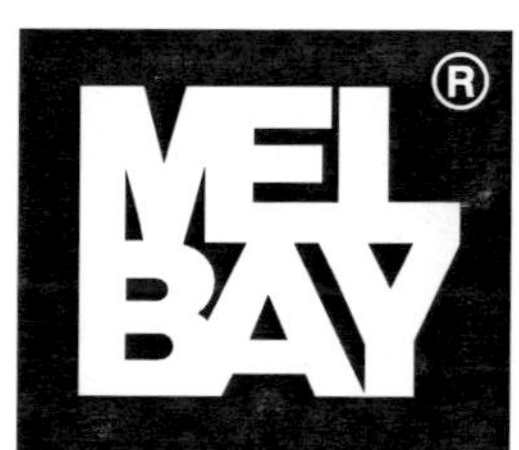

WWW.MELBAY.COM

Table of Contents

Fundamental Jazz Music Theory

The degrees of the C Major Scale:

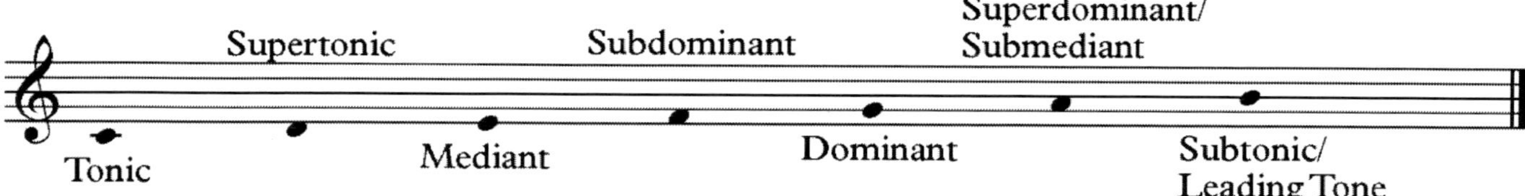

Triads formed on each degree of the major scale:

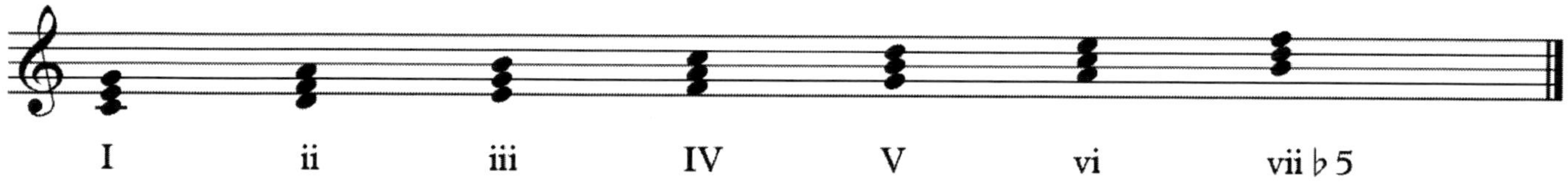

The chords of a ii^7-V^7-I progression can be found by stacking thirds on top of specific scale degrees in a given key. In the figure below the chords that participate in the ii^7-V^7-I progression are marked with boxes. Lower-case Roman numerals stand for minor chords and upper-case Roman numerals represent major chords.

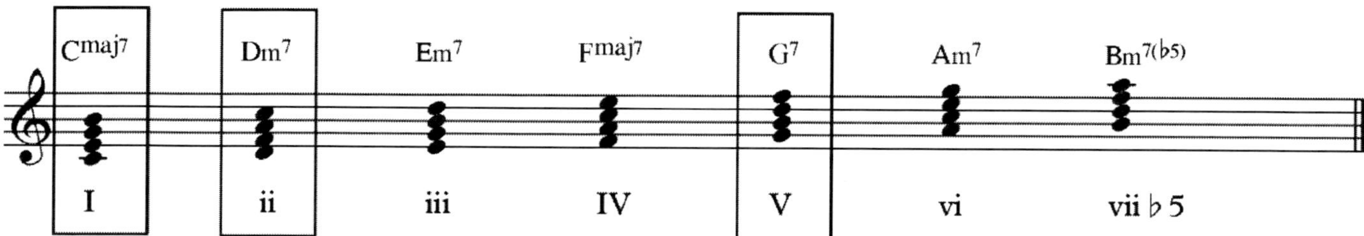

Any new notes that are added above the 7th of a given chord, such as 9^{ths}, 11^{ths}, and 13^{ths} are considered chord extensions. Extensions can occur in various shadings such as sharp 9^{ths}, flat 13^{ths}, etc. Specific conventions dictate which shadings may be used over a given chord quality, yet for the purposes of this book we are mostly concerned with the extensions occurring over minor seventh chords in the context of a major ii^7-V^7-I progression.

In jazz, many musicians think of chords as vertically organized scales. This concept, commonly referred to as *chord-scale theory*, also refers to the specific scales and modes that are used for any given chord. When stacking diatonic thirds on top of the note D, using pitches of the C major scale, the resulting structure is a Dm^{13} chord. This chord also includes all the pitches of the D Dorian mode, which is the default scale for this chord. Note that the Dm^{13} chord is derived from the second degree of the C major scale and has no sharps or flats.

An arpeggiated Dm^{13} chord The D Dorian mode

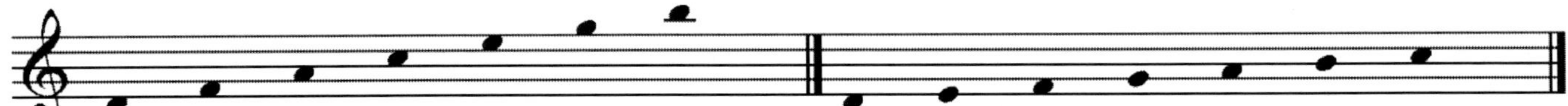

The 9th assumes the presence of the 7th, the 11th assumes the presence of the 7th and the 9th, the 13th assumes the presence of the 7th, 9th, and 11th, yet players of chordal instruments do not always include all chord tones and extensions in their voicings. Sometimes these omissions are a matter of personal taste, but with fretted instruments it is often impossible to include all the tones in an extended chord. The 5th and the root of the chord are often omitted as the 5th is common to both major and minor triads and the root can easily be played by a bassist. In contrast, the third of the chord is very important because it gives the chord its major or minor character.

The 13th is as far as the stacking of intervals of a third can be extended. Trying to go to a 15th would only lead back to the tonic. Besides creating a more interesting chord progression, the use of extensions gives both the composer and the improvising player more options as to the melody and improv resources that fit the chord progression.

The G^{7} chord, which is the V^{7} chord in a ii^{7}-V^{7}-I progression in C major, is derived from the fifth degree of the scale. The default scale that fits with and compliments the G^{7} chord is the G mixolydian mode, which exclusively consists of the pitches of the C major scale.

An arpeggiated G^{7} chord

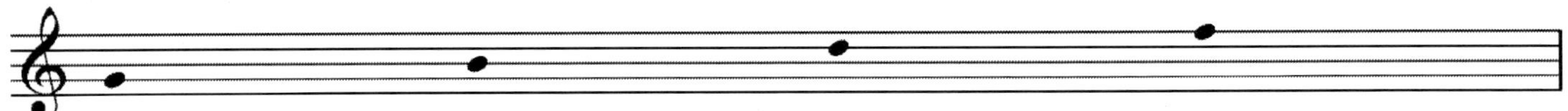

How to Use this Book

This book is based on a few fundamental ideas and objectives that can be arranged in the following two categories:

1) Strategies and exercises that are designed to provide you with a guided approach to improve your jazz improvisation skills, help you to develop a jazz vocabulary, increase your level of fluency and give you the tools to outline progressions clearly.

2) A core idea of this book is to make the most out of the least amount of material. Accordingly, systematically organized ideas are presented to enable you to have something to play in any situation.

All five of the strategies outlined in the table of contents stem from what can be heard on legendary jazz albums. Consequently, this is not a theoretical experiment but a hands-on way of learning jazz improvisation that is connected to the tradition. The book is clear enough to enable you to work on the material by yourself but having a teacher to guide you is always recommended. It's always beneficial to have someone to keep you accountable and coach you through your progress.

The fundamental idea underlying this book is to prepare you to be a fluent and well-versed improviser. Thus, the first strategy helps you to develop material starting on any note of the ii^7 chord (i.e., every note of the Dorian mode associated with the ii^7 chord prefacing every V^7 chord). This means that after practicing the exercises in this book you'll be able to start on any note of any ii^7 chord and have some material to play.

All exercises should be practiced in every key to ensure readiness when improvising. You do not have to practice all the licks in this book. Pick one from each subcategory to start with. For example, choose one lick that starts on the root of the ii^7 chord and practice it at various tempos and in different keys. Then move on to a lick that starts from the third of the ii^7 chord and so on. Don't practice only the licks that start from the root of the ii^7 chord before moving on. Variety is the key to making art and improving your fluency as an improviser. If you practice two ascending licks, make sure you practice some descending ideas next.

Here are some examples of licks to get you started:

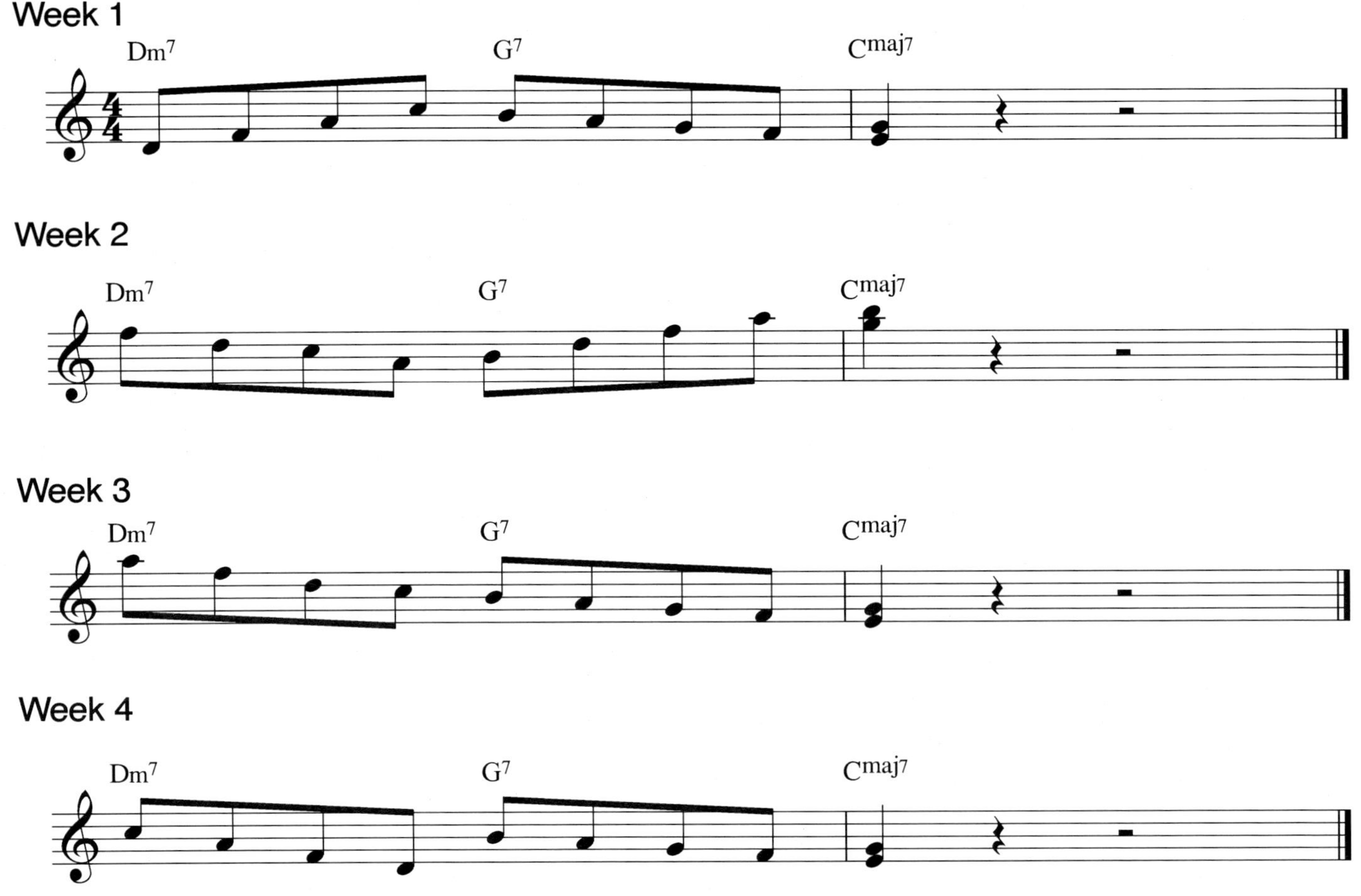

Always keep variety in mind when practicing. Remember that these licks are examples – you are always encouraged to transcribe and invent your own.

The licks in this book are diatonic for the most part – meaning that the licks do not contain pitch material that is foreign to the given key. There are several reasons for this: 1) Chromatic (non-diatonic) material is reserved for a potential later volume; 2) there is plenty of material to work on within the realm of diatonic licks; 3) chromaticism is introduced in strategy two of this book; and 4) the tenet of this volume is to present the most coherent and basic materials such as arpeggiated ii^7, V^7, and I^{maj7} chords as well as diatonic modes.

All licks in this book are short ii^7-V^7s. The chapters on combination and tritone substitution show you how to make longer ii^7-V^7s with the material you have already practiced.

The section on rhythmic variations will help you diversify your practice. You should pick a different rhythm whenever you get bored with the one you've been using for a while. You might also implement some sort of regimen that forces you to incorporate rhythmic diversity into your practicing. For instance, use one specific rhythm for week one and then switch to another rhythm for week two, etc.

The exercises in this book are not transposed into every key. It is a crucial component of your practice to develop the skill of being able to transpose on the spot. Without this ability, it is nearly impossible to play jazz at a high level. The truth behind being a great performer is simple – you must work harder than anyone and practice more efficiently. No teacher can give you a magic exercise that will turn you into a genius. Slow repetitions and strict organization are essential.

Some helpful reminders and mantras:

- Always use a metronome or a reference to metronomic time when practicing.
- Set daily, weekly, and monthly goals.
- When you have problems motivating yourself, think about musical scenarios in which you will need the specific skills you are developing.
- A little work every day is better than a lot occasionally.
- Practice how you want to sound.
- Work with a vision in mind.
- There will always be someone better than you, but everybody has a story to tell that's worth hearing.
- Through efficient practice, you can program and condition your brain and body to execute complex and multilayered skills effortlessly.
- Repetition is everything; automate things until you don't have to think about them.
- Start by practicing slow and increase the tempo incrementally.
- Great time starts with your fingers and an even technique - scales!
- Remember the 3 Ts: **T**ime – **T**one – playing in **T**une.
- Make sure you have performance and playing opportunities that require practice. If you don't have people calling you, set up a session yourself.
- Always try to sound the best you can.
- Be the best version of yourself you can be.
- "To play a wrong note is insignificant; to play without passion is inexcusable."
  Beethoven

Strategy 1 – Developing Jazz Vocabulary and Fluency

The ii^7-V^7-I progression is omnipresent in jazz; hence it is essential to have material ready to improvise over this progression in every key and tempo. You must be able to start on any note of the ii^7 chord. It's an added benefit that all the pitches in the Dorian mode are consonant when played over the ii^7 chord.

The resolution of a line imbues it with a specific character. In this book, when resolving to the I chord, two options are often provided since the preceding note occurring over the V^7 chord may resolve upward or downward. Offering two options for resolving a given line diversifies the material and will train your ear to vary it.

Starting on the Root of the ii⁷ Chord

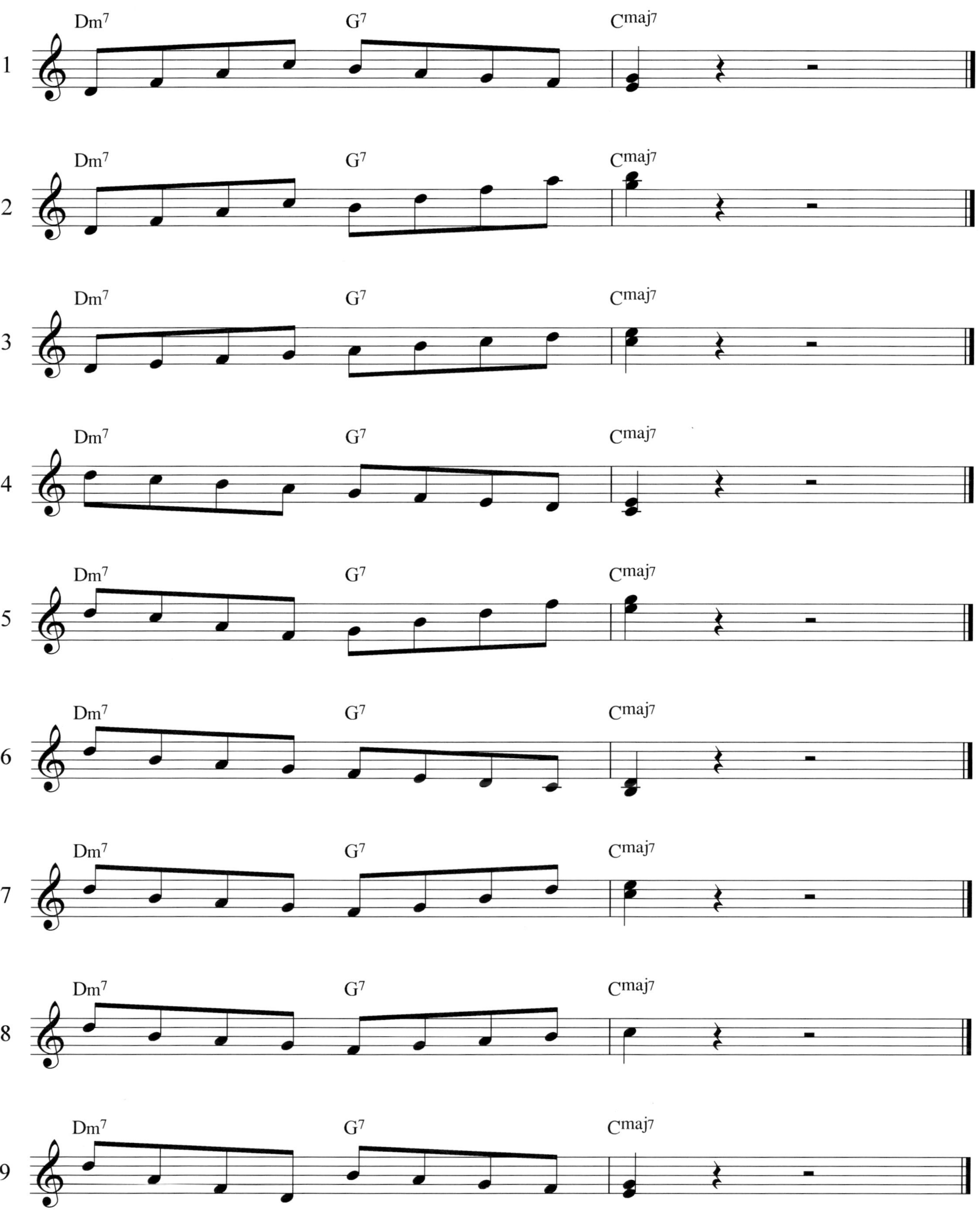

Starting on the 3rd of the ii7 Chord

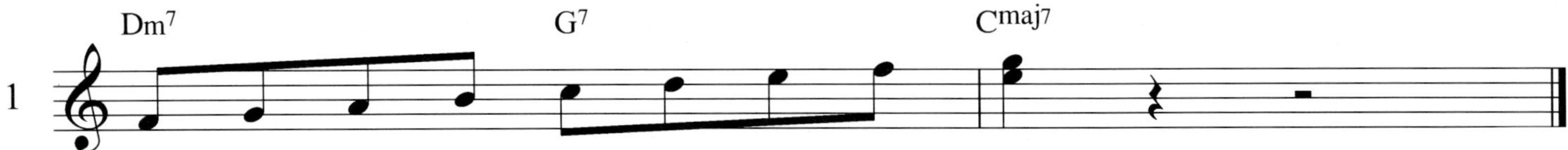

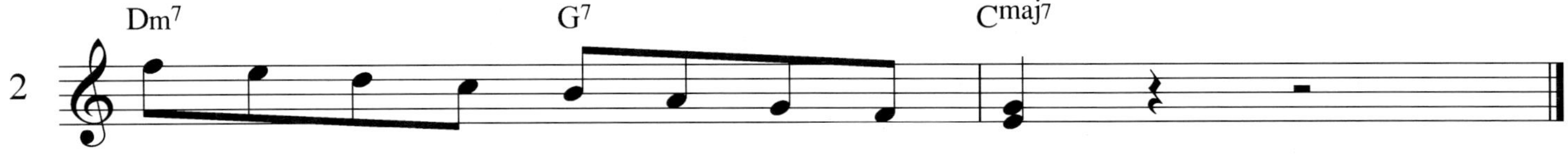

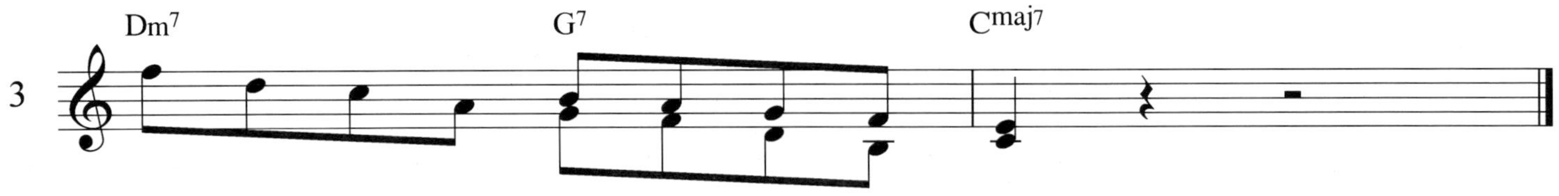

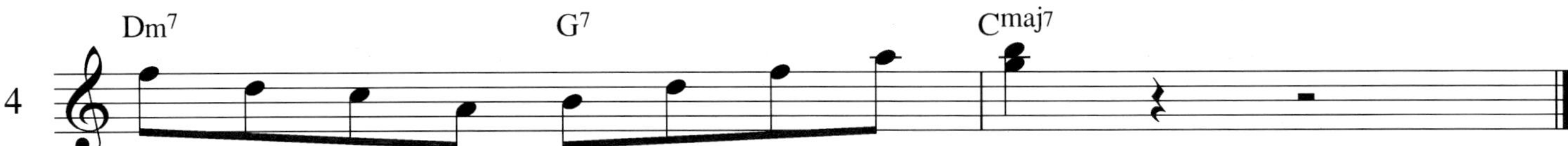

Starting on the 5th of the ii⁷ Chord

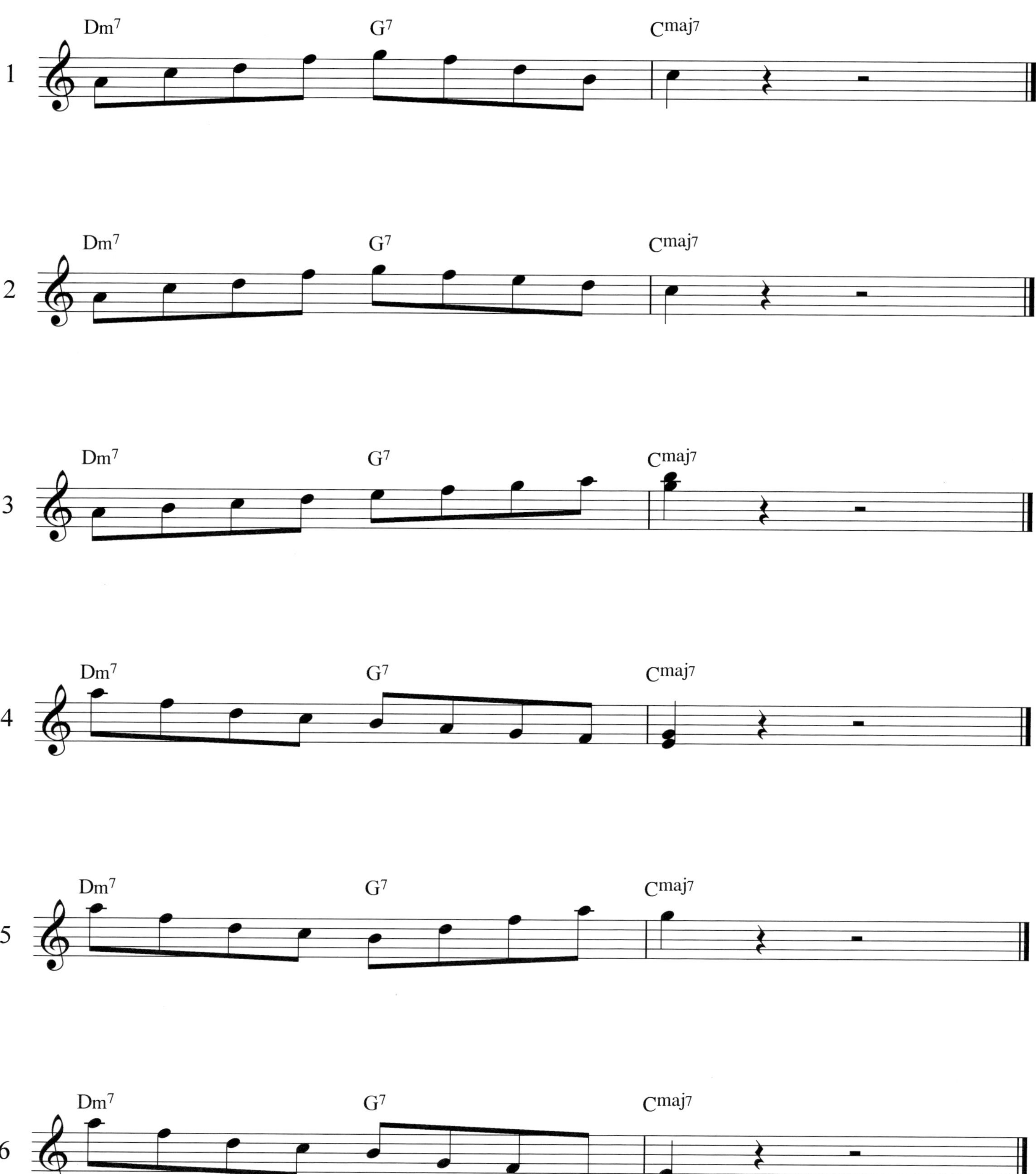

Starting on the 7th of the ii7 Chord

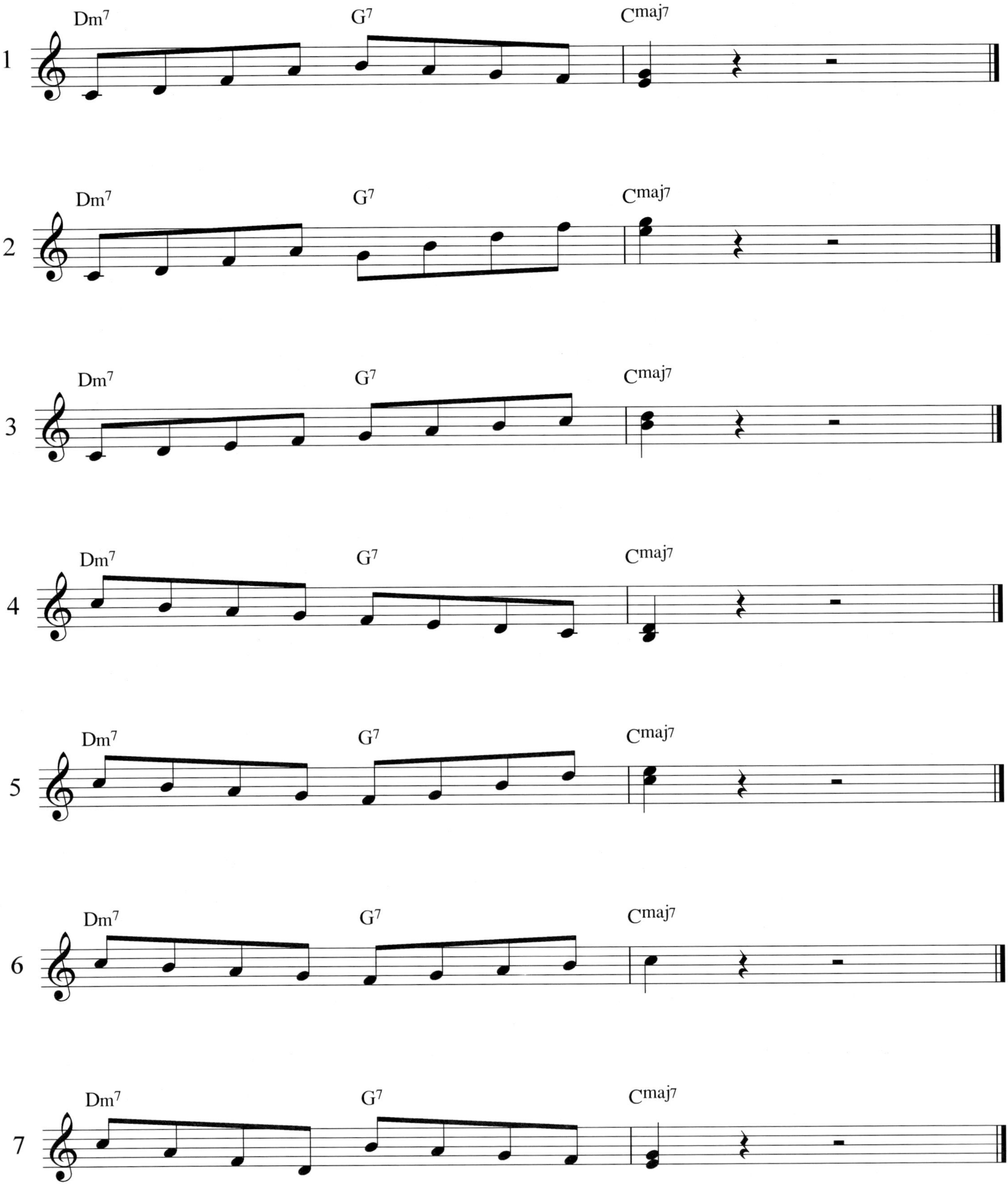

Starting on the 9th of the Extended ii7 Chord

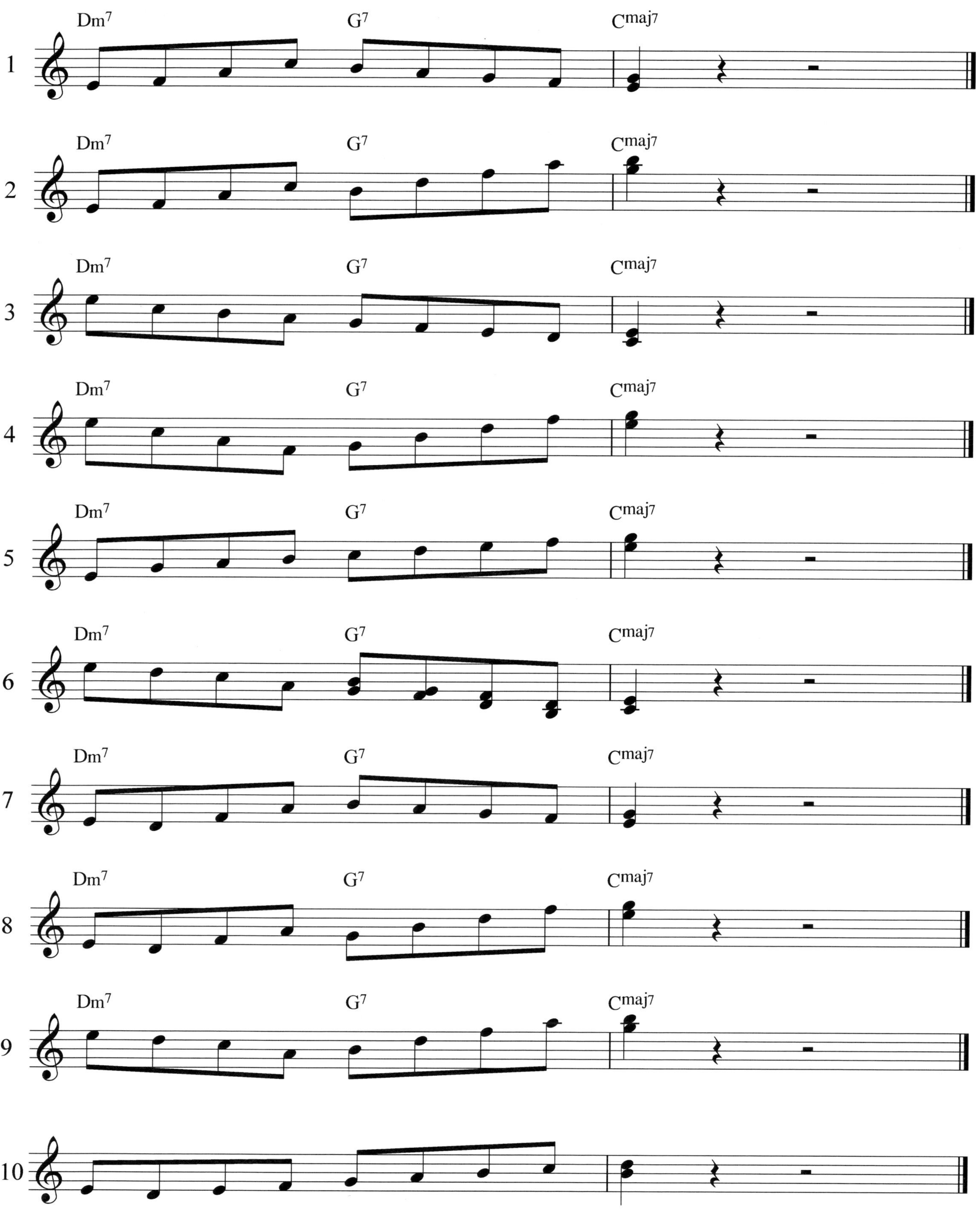

Starting on the 11th of the Extended ii7 Chord

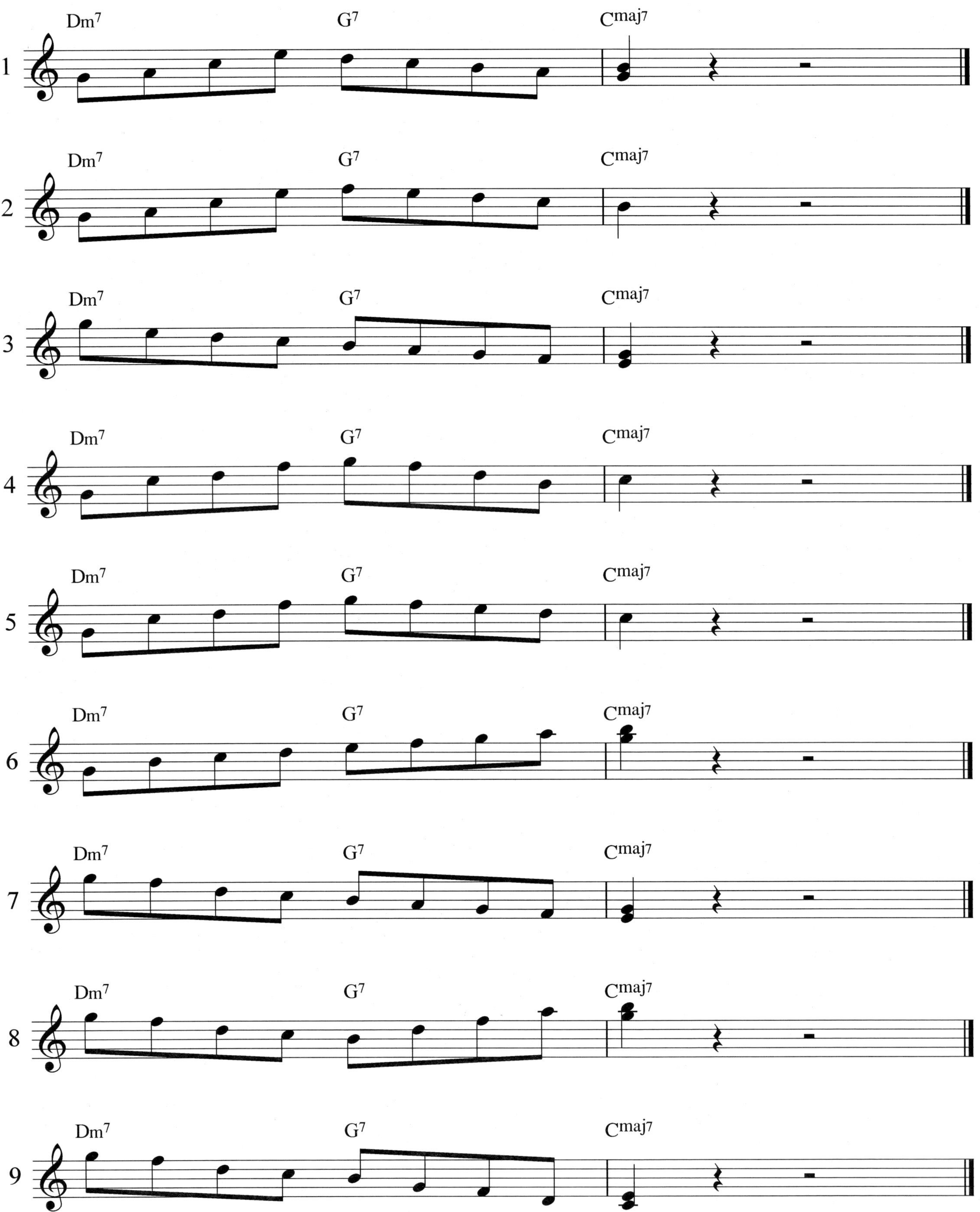

Starting on the 13th of the Extended ii7 Chord

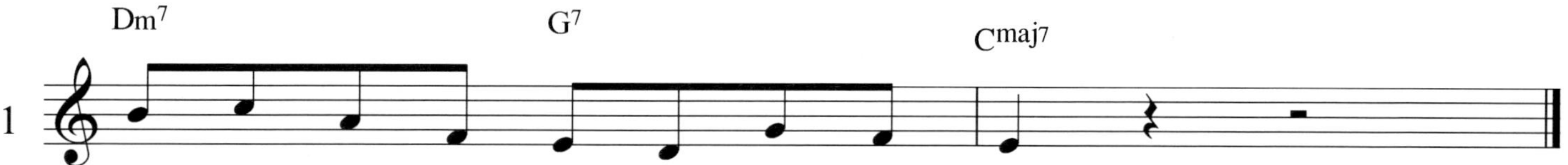

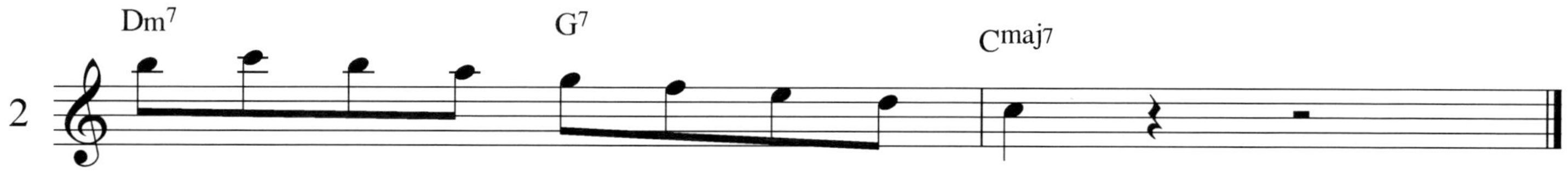

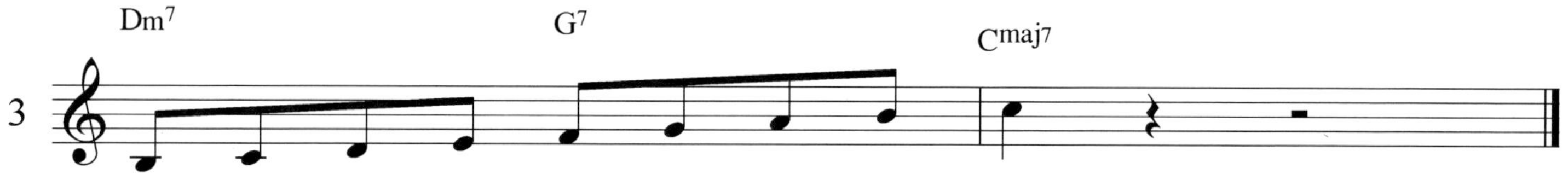

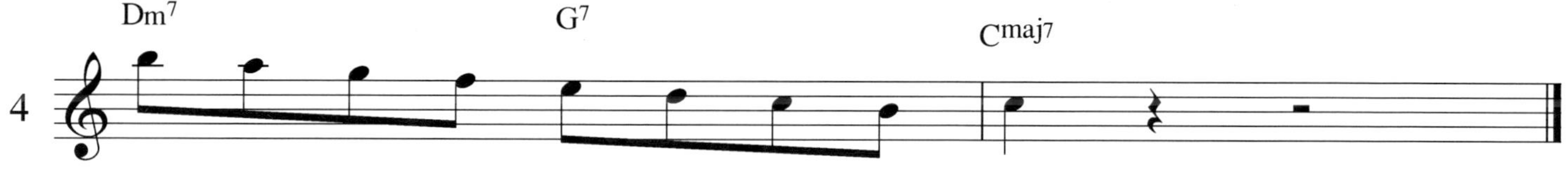

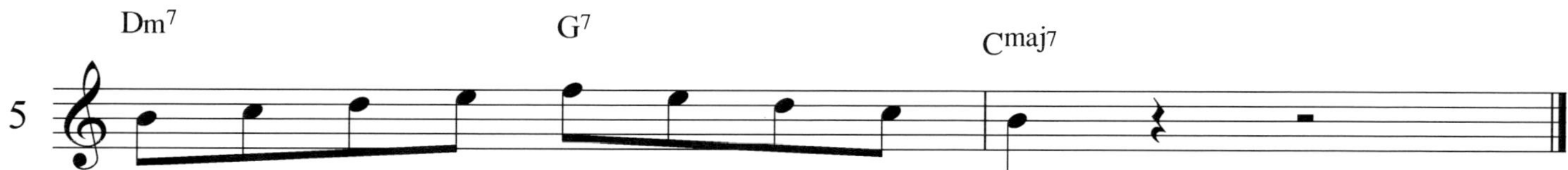

Rhythmic Variations

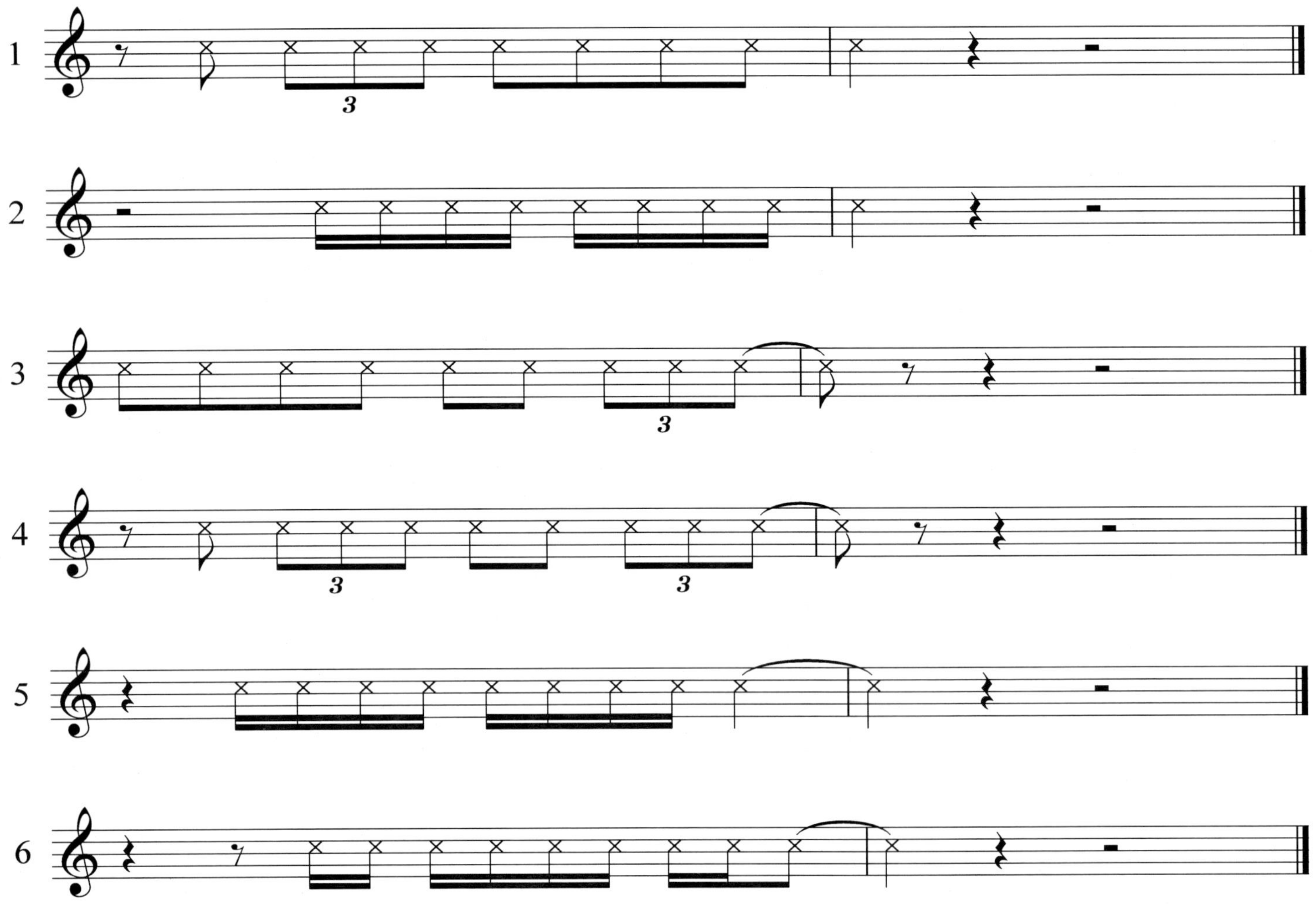

1

2

3

4

5

6

Practice the licks with these rhythms and come up with your own.

Example:

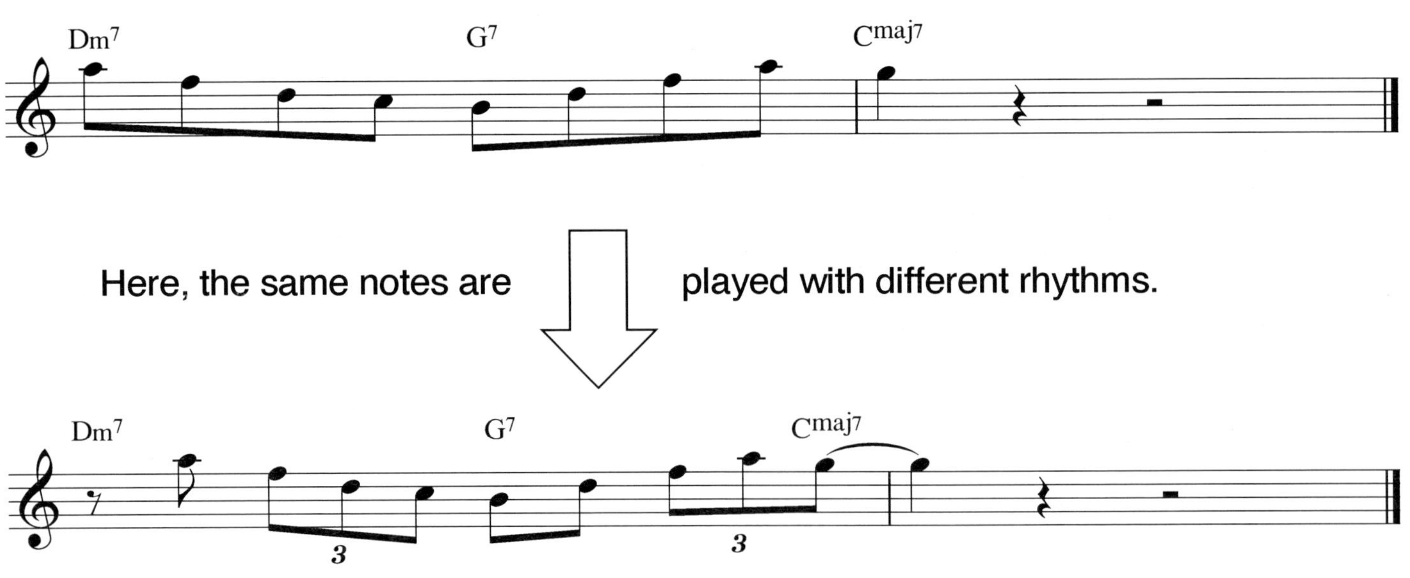

Major Chord Licks

Incorporate these major chord licks after or while practicing the ii^7-V^7 licks. You can also practice the ii^7-V^7 licks without resolving to the given major-chord resolution pitches or practice these major chord licks independently.

Starting on the Root

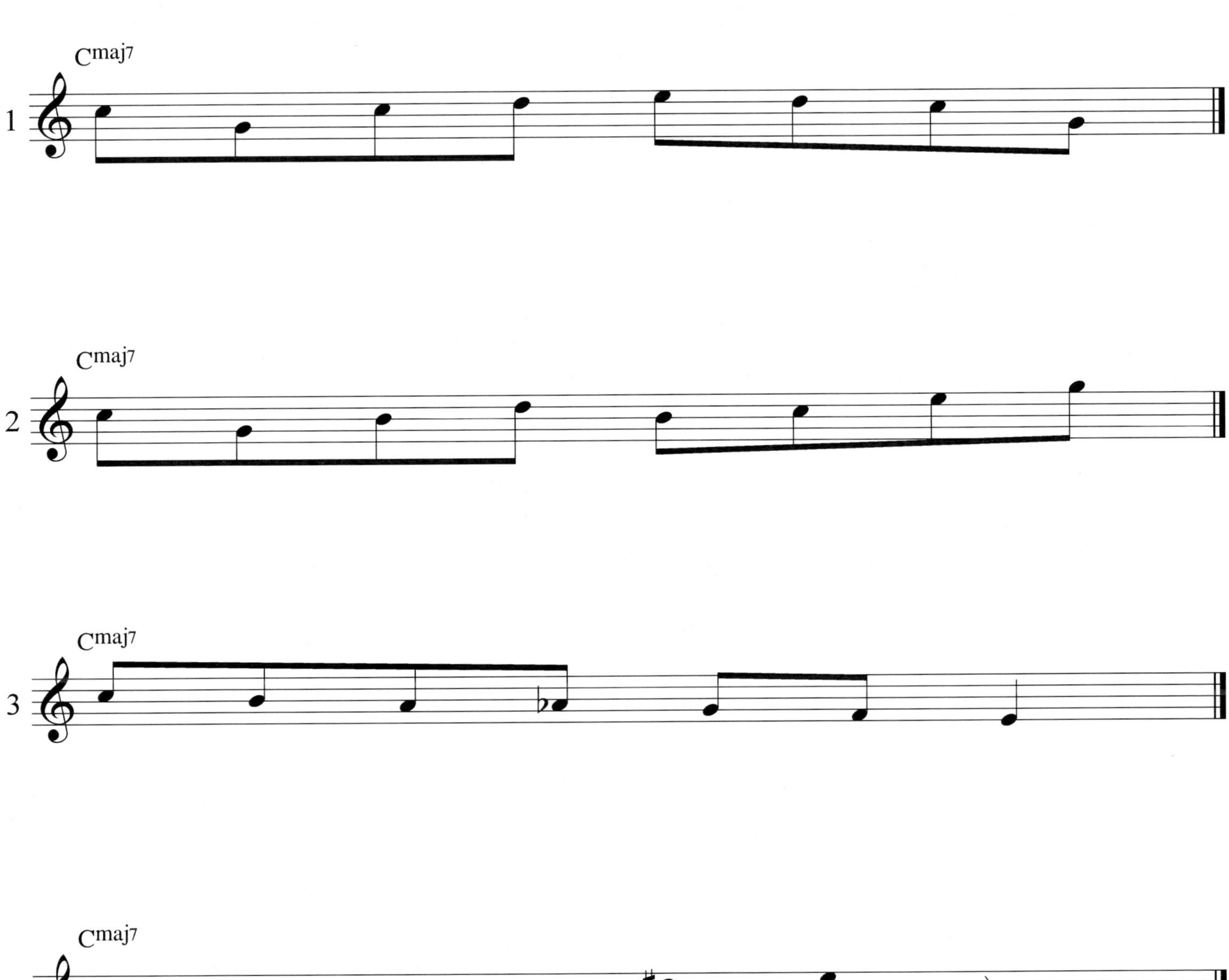

Starting on the 3rd

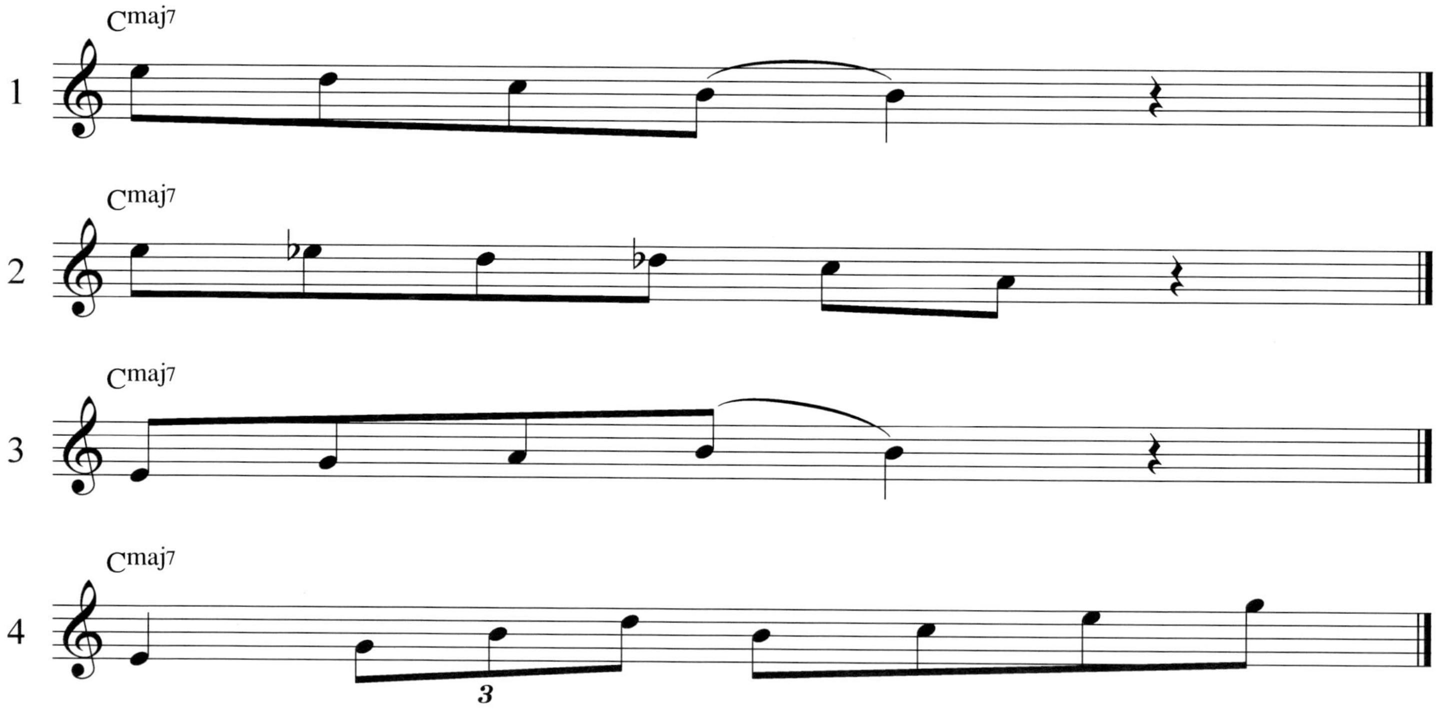

Starting on the 5th

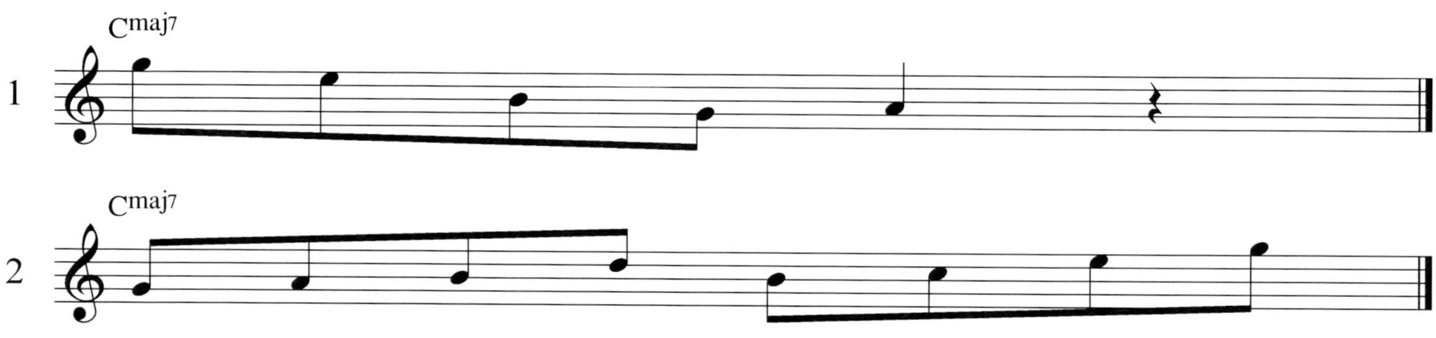

Starting on the 7th

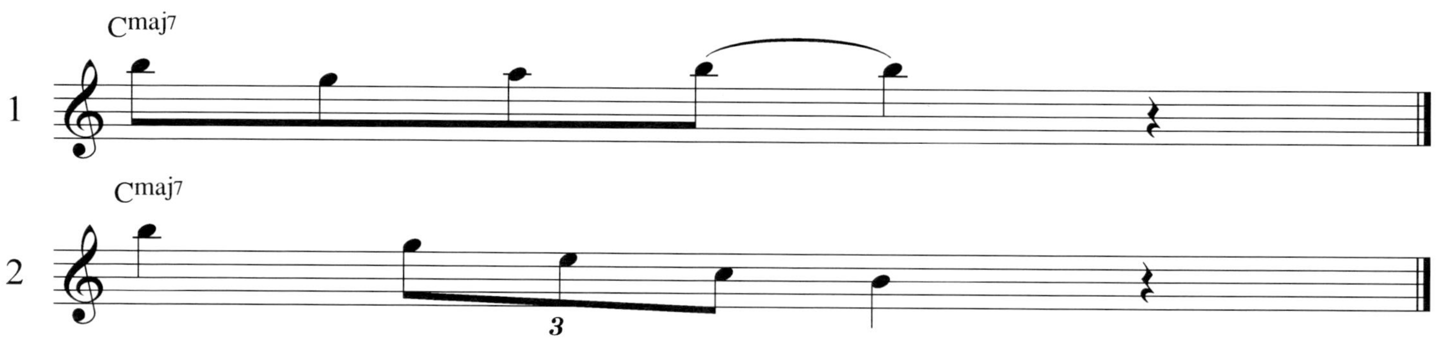

Strategy 2 – Creating Longer ii^7-V^7 Licks Through Tritone Substitution

A tritone is an interval consisting of three consecutive whole tones (six semitones).

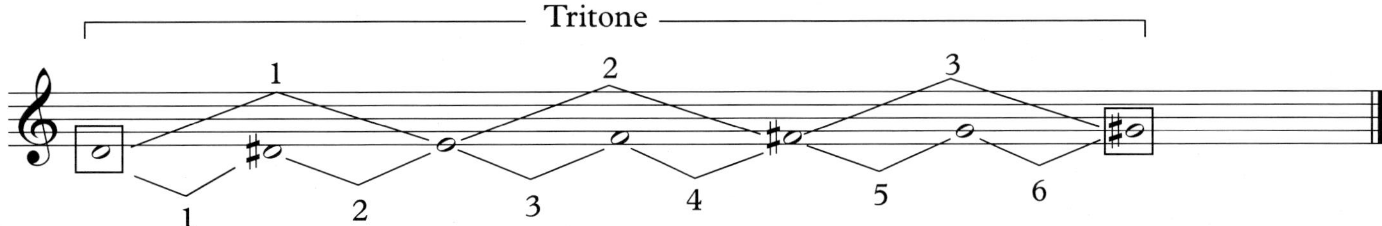

Tritones are also referred to as augmented fourth or diminished fifth.

Tritone as augmented 4th Tritone as diminished 5th

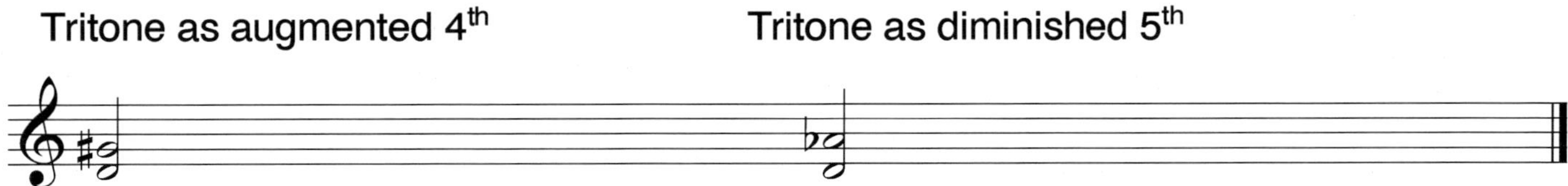

You can create longer ii^7-V^7 licks by combining two short ii^7-V^7 ideas that are a tritone apart. This strategy is related to one of the core ideas behind this book – making the most of the least amount of material possible. The concept of tritone substitution enables this strategy.

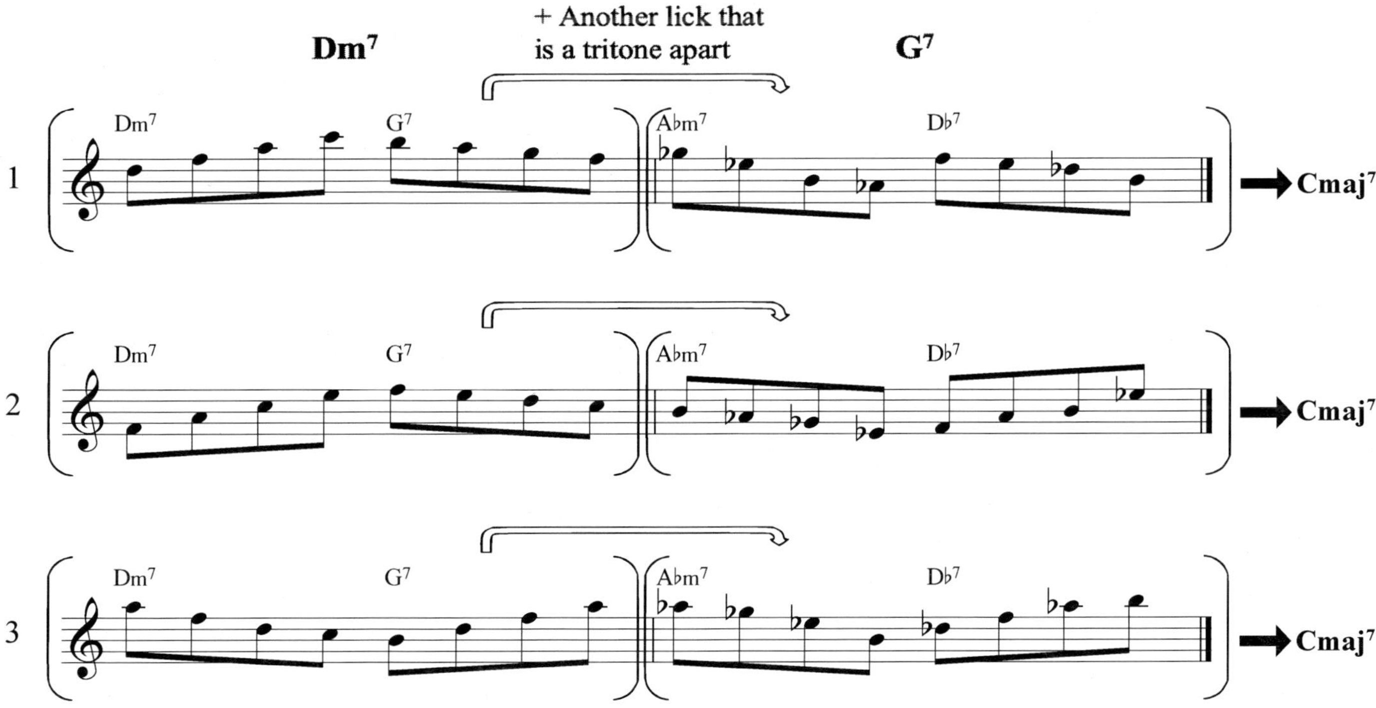

Tritone Substitution

The fundamental idea behind tritone substitution is the fact that dominant seventh chords which are a tritone apart share the same 3rds and 7ths, e.g.: The third and seventh of C^7 are E and B♭, which are identical to the seventh and third of $F♯^7$. Accordingly, $F♯^7$ can stand in for or be switched out with C^7 and vice-versa.

Common tones in two V^7 chords whose roots form tritones.

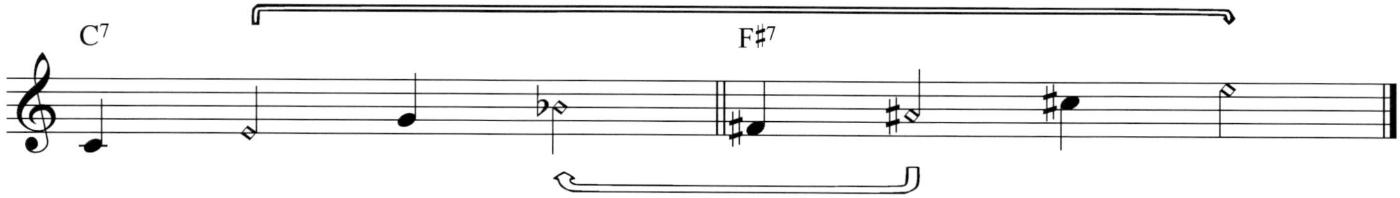

Strategy 3 – Combination

Creating New Licks Through Combination

The following three licks are from the section "Licks Starting on the 5th of the ii7 Chord." They only serve as examples. You can combine any of the licks from this book in this manner. To distinguish between ii7 chord material and V7 chord material, the ii7 chord portions are boxed while the V7 segments are marked with brackets. In addition, the specific units are labeled with capital letters, indicating whether they belong to the ii7 (A) or the V7 (B) chord.

Here are three main licks that can be used as source material:

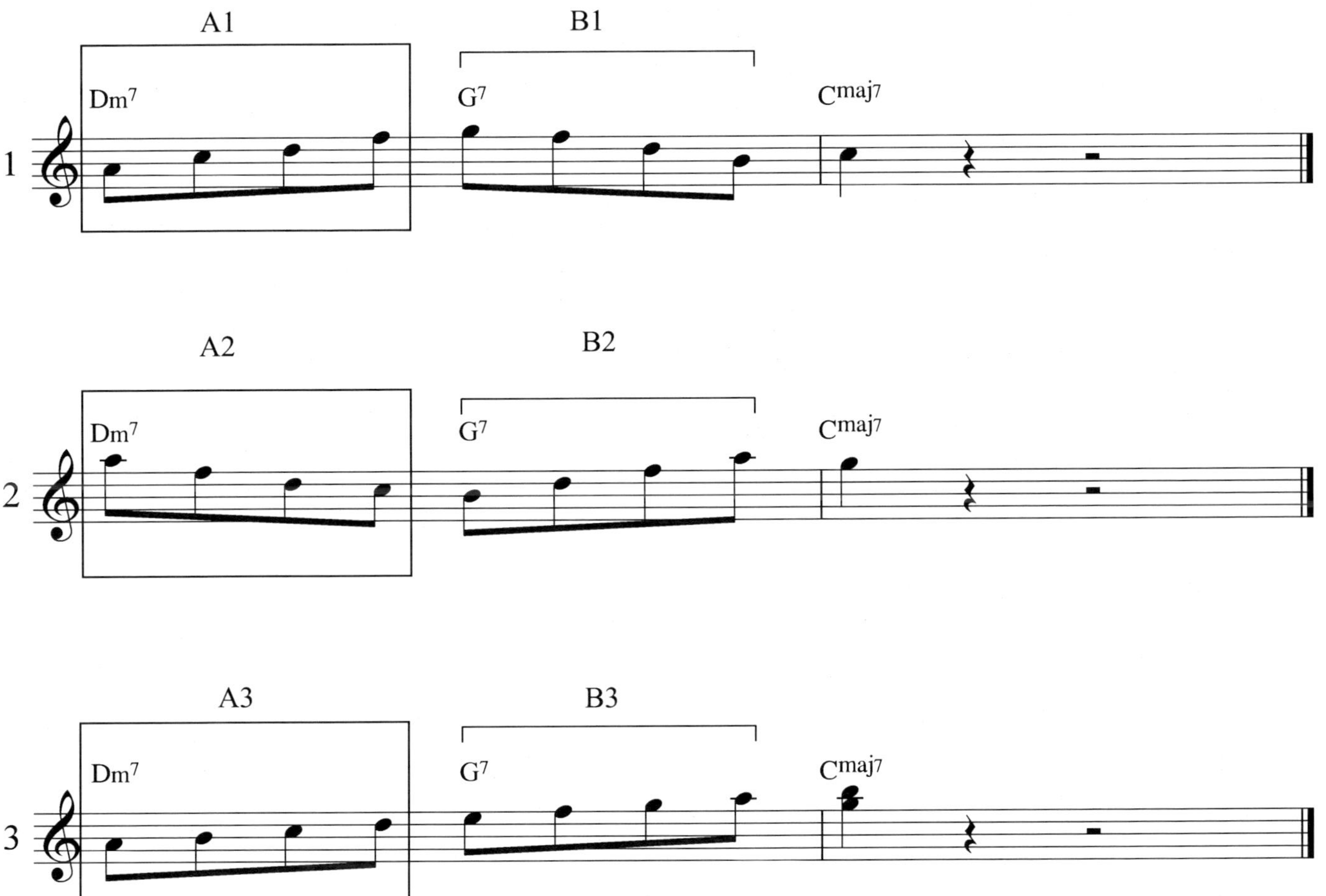

Now the individual units can be recombined to generate new licks: A1+B2, A1+B3, A2+B1, A2+B3, A3+B1, and A3+B2:

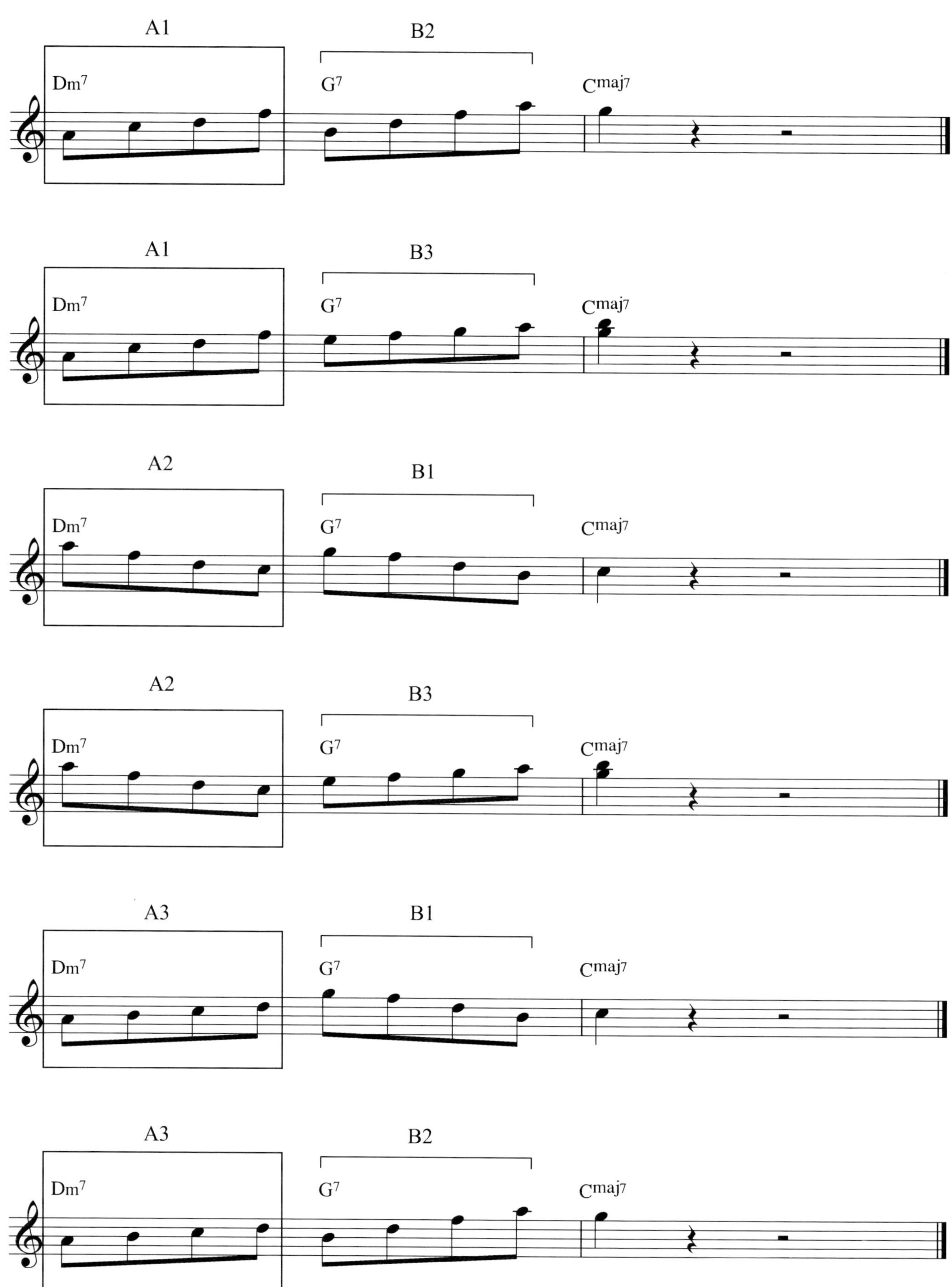

Creating Long ii^7-V^7 Licks Through Combination

Here, two short ii^7-V^7 licks are combined to create one longer ii^7-V^7 lick.

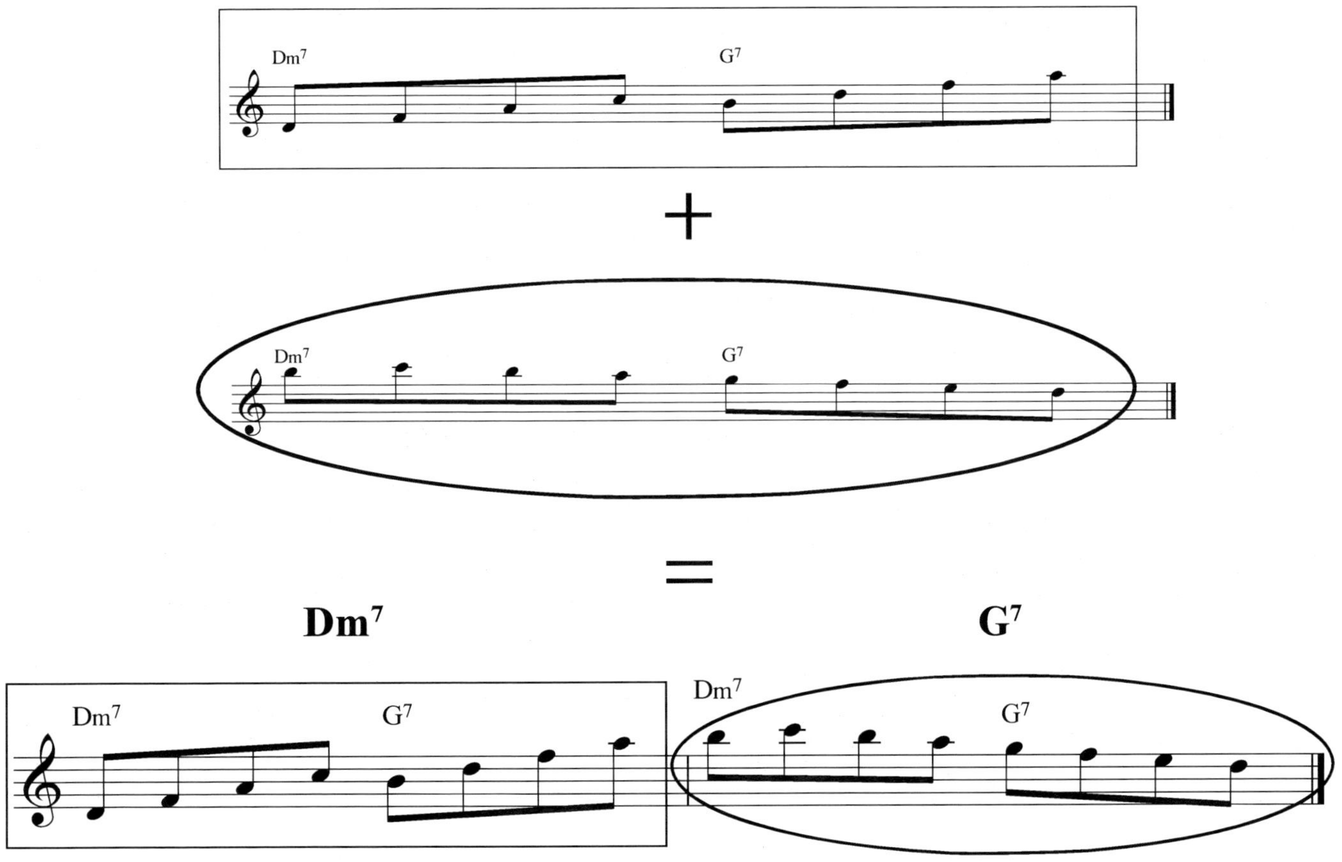

This strategy can also be used to generate double-time material.:

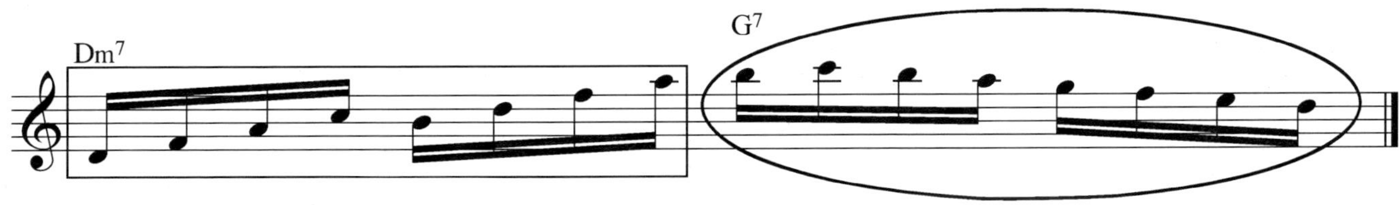

Experiment with different combinations to discover the ones you would like to incorporate in your own playing. You will see that some of them work better that others.

Strategy 4 – Sample Exercises for Developing Fluency

String together any of the licks from this book and practice them using the following nine transposition paths:

Transposition Path	Sample Location
1) Circle of 4ths/5ths	B section of Rhythm Changes
2) Ascending chromatically	"Moment's Notice" by John Coltrane
3) Descending chromatically	"Stable Mates" by Benny Golson
4) Ascending in whole steps	ii^7-V^7-iii^7-V^7 progressions as found in the A sections of "Perdido" by Juan Tizol
5) Descending in whole steps	"Straight Street" by John Coltrane
6) Ascending in minor thirds	"Lazy Bird" by John Coltrane
7) Descending in minor thirds	Harold Mabern's and Eric Alexander's arrangement of "Almost Like Being in Love" by Frederick Loewe and Alan Jay Lerner.
8) Ascending in major thirds	The interlude of John Coltrane's arrangement of "But Not for Me" by George and Ira Gershwin
9) Descending in major thirds	"Alone Together" by Arthur Schwartz and Howard Dietz in measures nine through ten of the A section.

- You will discover that you need to master this material to function well in various performance situations.
- On the following pages I have provided some sample exercises that demonstrate how the ii^7-V^7 licks should be strung together and practiced.

Sample Exercise 1: Ascending Chromatically

Take any lick or group of licks from this book and practice them in this fashion.

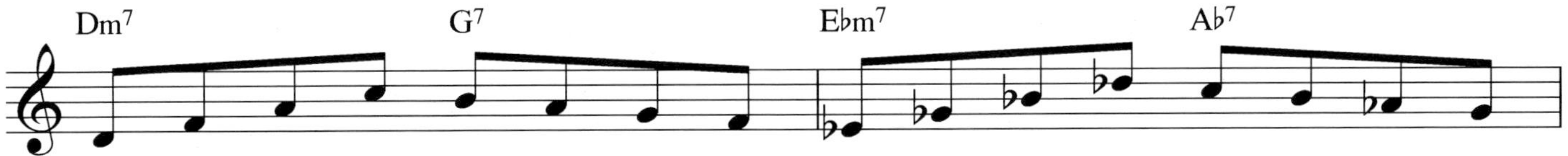

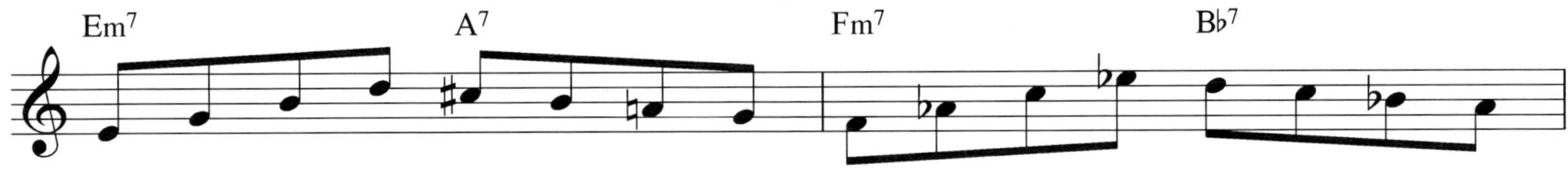

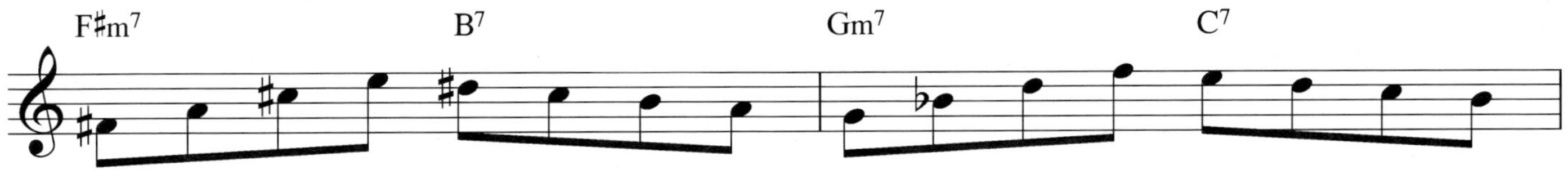

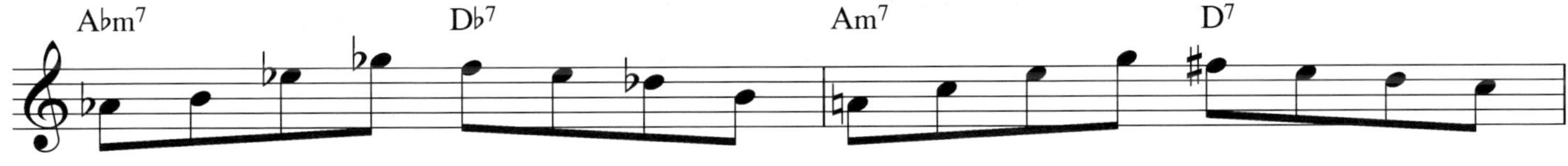

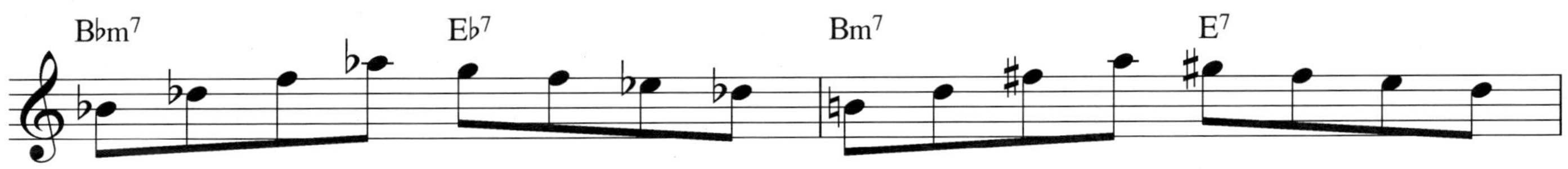

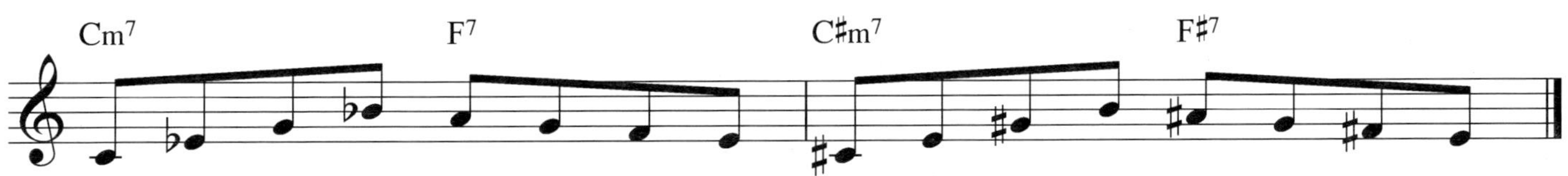

Sample Exercise 2: Ascending & Descending in Whole Steps

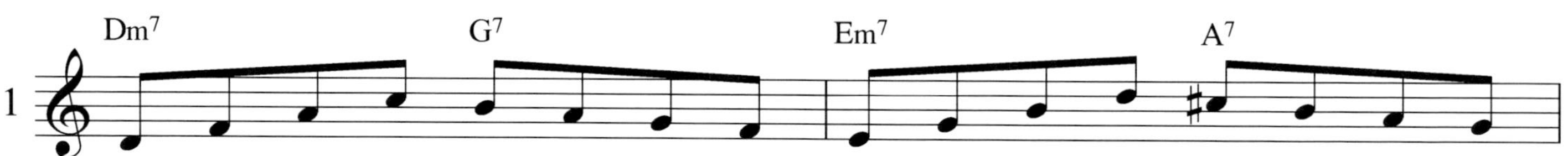

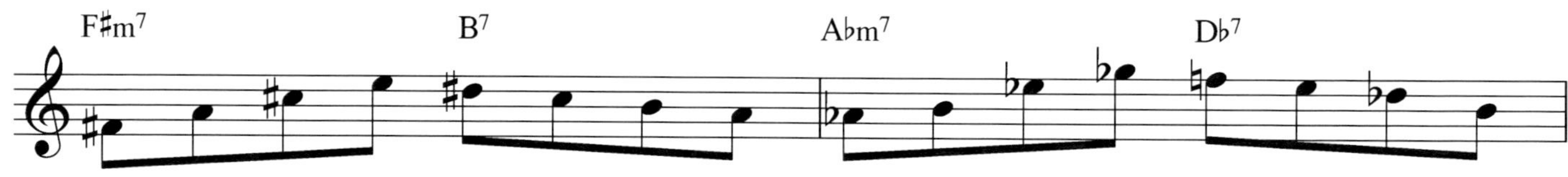

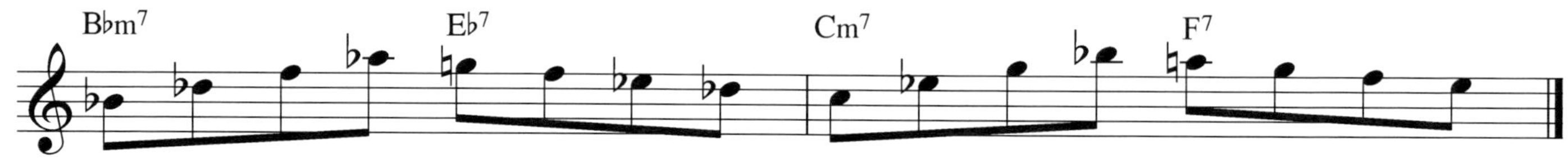

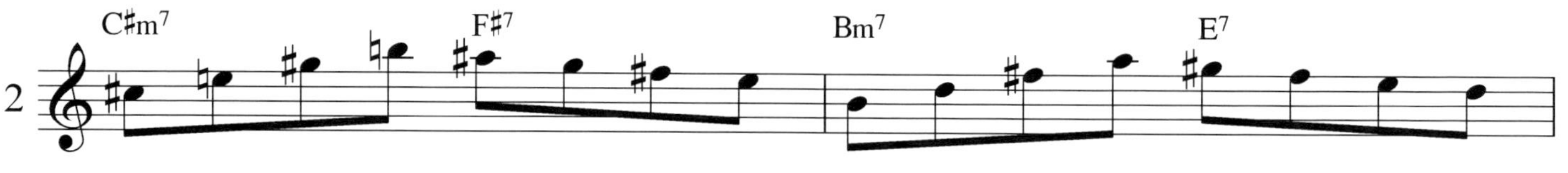

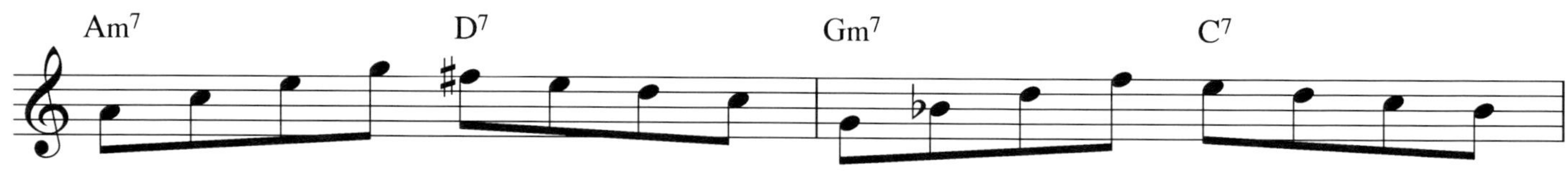

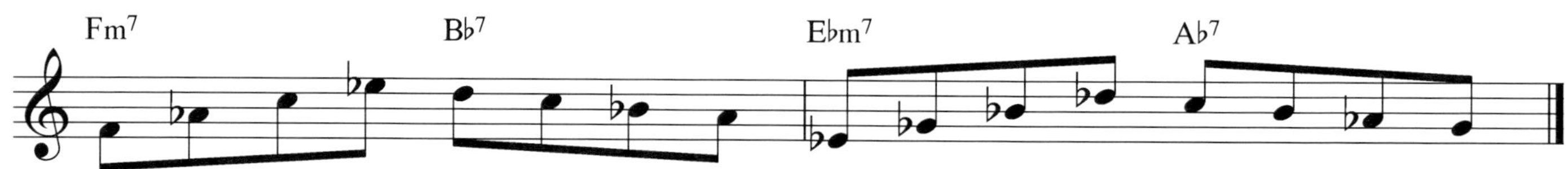

Sample Exercise 3: Ascending in Major Thirds

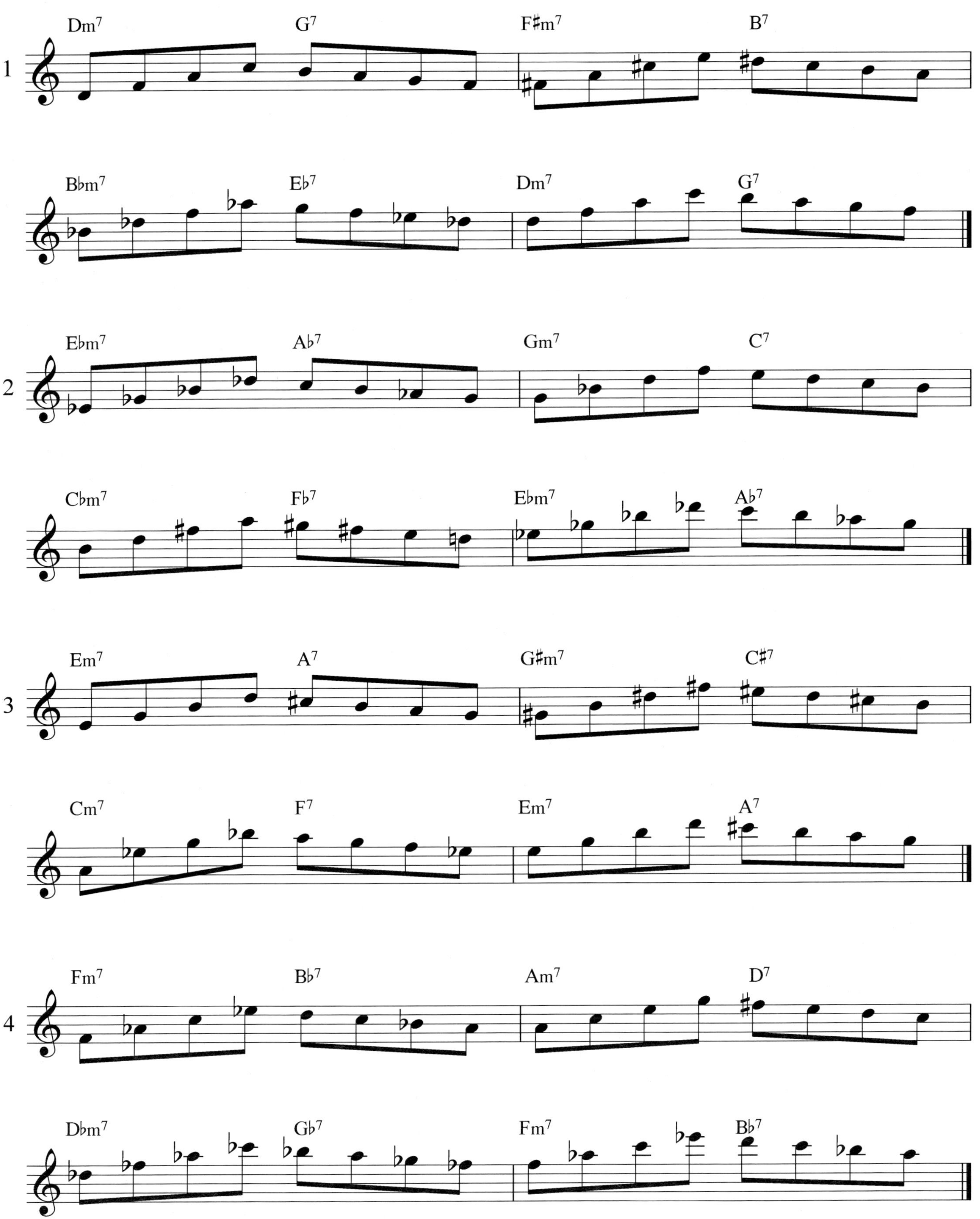

Strategy 5 – Implementation and Application

The "Plug-in Method"

While you practice some of the ideas from this book, it is important to work on applying the materials to real playing scenarios. For this method, you need to choose a song, a lick, and a metronome or play-along recording. When you have everything ready, pick a specific measure or set of measures over which you'll "plug-in" the same lick every single chorus.

This method will:

1) Strengthen your sense of form
2) Increase your fluency and readiness
3) Improve your ability to express harmony and rhythm clearly
4) Force you to construct musically coherent statements using limited specific material
5) Make you better at finding ways of expressing yourself.

Once you feel comfortable implementing your chosen lick chorus after chorus, proceed by playing variations of the lick by changing the rhythm, tone, dynamics, or articulation.

Example:

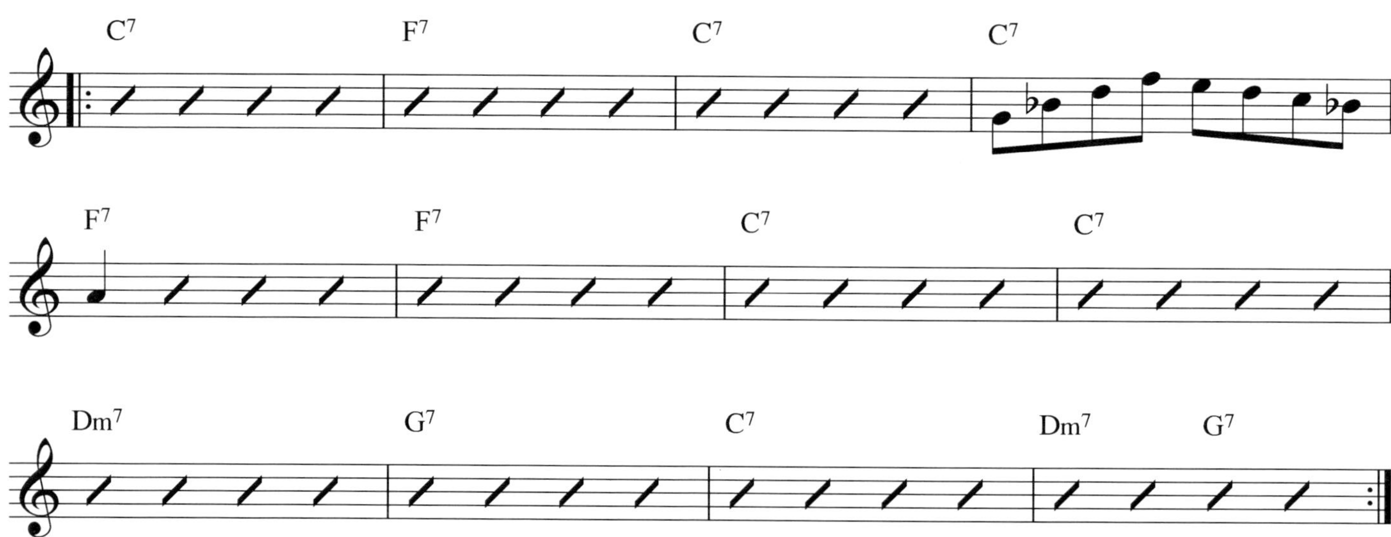

Below is a blues in C which you can repeat until you feel comfortable playing your chosen lick, each time in the same location. You can improvise for the remainder of the form (slash marks) or work on other specific improv techniques. After a while you might try displacing the lick rhythmically by shifting it back or forth one or several eighth notes.

Once you have mastered the first step of the exercise, make it more challenging by:

1) Implementing additional licks,

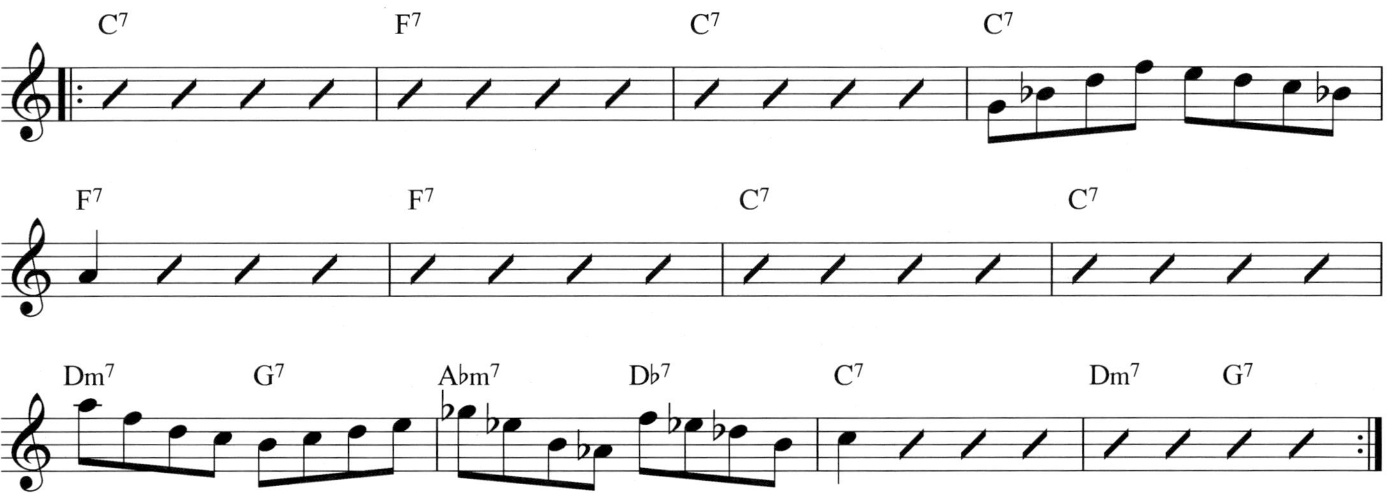

or...

2) Playing every chorus in a different key and/or

3) Increasing the tempo, or

4) Playing a different song.

The "Building Block Method"

This method of implementation also requires a song, a set of licks, and a metronome or play-along recording. Akin to building blocks, which can be combined in many ways, this exercise challenges you to use your material in various combinations. There are several degrees of difficulty that you can apply to this method:

Begin with a single lick, then add two licks, three licks, and finally four licks.

1) For the first level of the "Building Block Method, "play the given lick over every single measure. If you play a wind instrument, pick places to breathe before you begin.

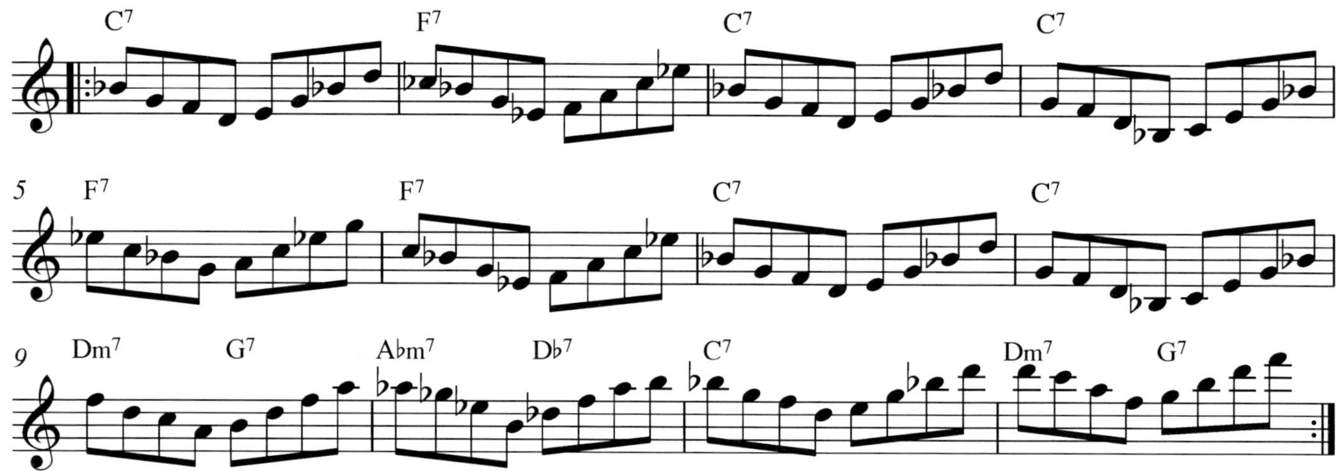

2) Once you have applied the elementary level of the "Building Block Method" to several songs, keys, and tempos, you can start to work with two licks in this fashion. Since we are working with multiple licks now, we must account for the various permutations. Accordingly, your two licks should not only be practiced in the original sequence of A followed by B but also in reverse order with B followed by A.

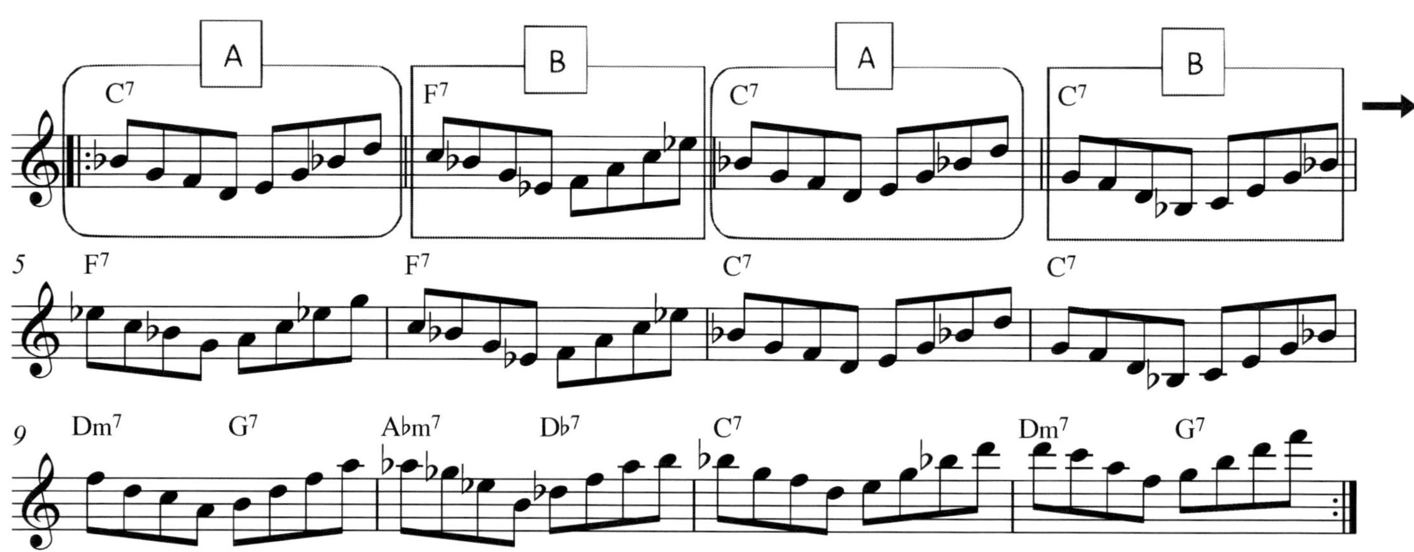

The more types of licks you work with using this method, the more permutations you will have to incorporate in your improvisations.

1 Lick with no permutations
2 Licks = 2 permutations [A, B] and [B, A]
3 Licks = 6 permutations [A-B-C]; [A-C-B]; [B-A-C]; [B-C-A]; [C-A-B]; [C-B-A]
4 Licks = 24 permutations!

The more licks you implement in this way, the more this exercise will sound like a complete piece of music. This is remarkable, considering that we began with one and two-bar phrases.

About the Author

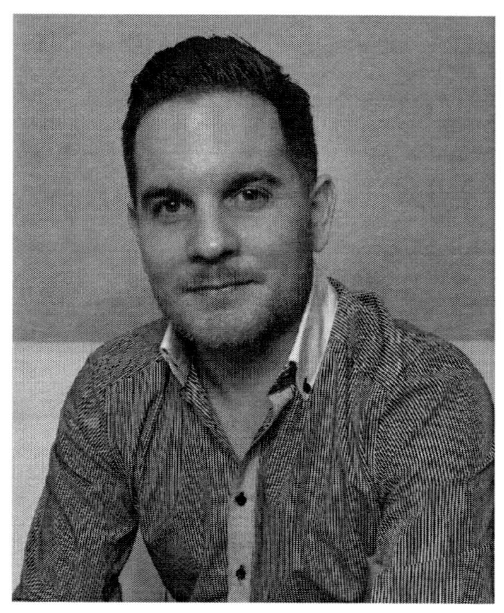

Austrian tenor saxophonist, composer, and musicologist Dr. Lukas Gabric (b. 1987) is hailed by Thomas Gansch and Joel Frahm as a "master musician" with "breathtaking tenor virtuosity" and has already made a mark on the international jazz scene. His performance and pedagogical activities have taken him to the USA, Germany, Italy, Switzerland, Hungary, Spain, Slovenia, China, South Korea, Mongolia, and Brazil.

Throughout his formative years, Dr. Gabric was selected as a member of the *European Generations Unit* at the biannual Festival in Frauenfeld, Switzerland in 2012. The adjudicators included the jazz icons Louis Hayes, Peter Washington, and David Hazeltine. In 2013 he was a semifinalist in the Thelonious Monk Competition in Washington D.C. In 2014 he won the Best Soloist Award and the Audience Choice Award at the Getxo Jazz Festival in Spain and received the third prize in the finals of the North American Saxophone Alliance Competition in Urbana-Champaign, Illinois. In 2016 Dr. Gabric was awarded the Herb Alpert Composer's Award by the American Society of Composers, Authors, and Publishers (ASCAP) for his composition "Fire Dance." In 2018 he received the Cultural Distinction Award and *Bruno Gironcoli Award* from his hometown of Villach (Austria), enabling him to produce his album *Labor of Love*, which received positive reviews in eight countries.

Dr. Gabric received a Post-Graduate Artist Diploma from the Juilliard School in New York, where he was a faculty member between 2014-2021. In addition, he holds a Ph.D. in musicology from The City College of New York, where he served as an adjunct lecturer between 2012-2020. He has also taught masterclasses and lectures at universities around the globe, published ten method books, several musicological articles, and other educational resources. For his role as a pedagogue and mentor, he was awarded the "Extraordinary Dedication and Achievement in Teaching Distinction" by the American Protégé International Competition at Carnegie Hall in 2019 and received a "Recognition for his Contribution to Excellence in Music Pedagogy" from the *Music & Stars* International Competition in 2021. In addition, he has organized the *Carinthian International Jazz Award* saxophone competition since 2018, which has attracted competitors from 40 countries. Dr. Gabric's solo album, *Double Standard*, released through Alessa Records in 2022, consists entirely of original compositions.